David and Goliath

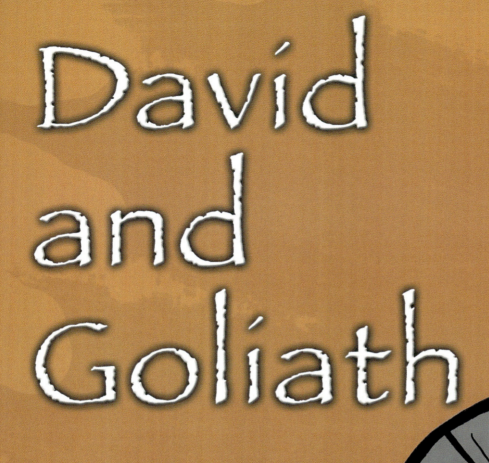

Written and Illustrated
by Gwenn Huot

To order additional copies of this book, contact:
Xlibris
844-714-8691
www.Xlibris.com
Orders@Xlibris.com

ISBN: Softcover 978-1-4363-6839-1
       EBook   978-1-6641-4912-0

Print information available on the last page

Rev. date: 12/18/2020

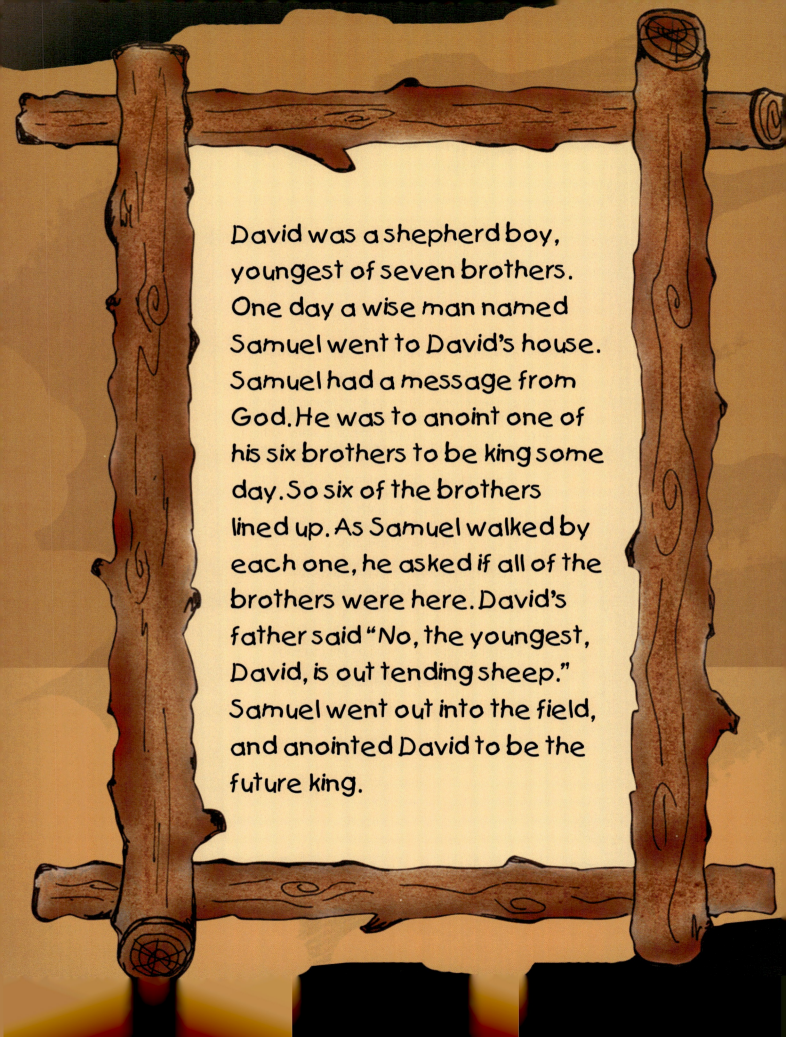

David was a shepherd boy, youngest of seven brothers. One day a wise man named Samuel went to David's house. Samuel had a message from God. He was to anoint one of his six brothers to be king some day. So six of the brothers lined up. As Samuel walked by each one, he asked if all of the brothers were here. David's father said "No, the youngest, David, is out tending sheep." Samuel went out into the field, and anointed David to be the future king.

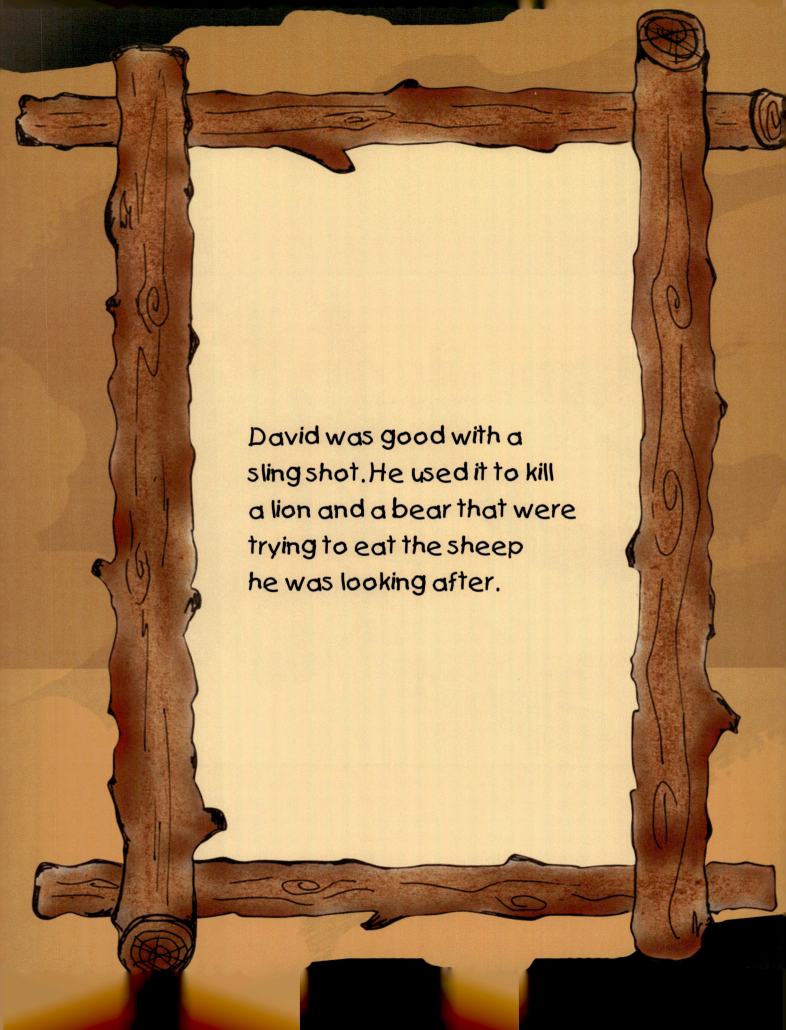

David was good with a
sling shot. He used it to kill
a lion and a bear that were
trying to eat the sheep
he was looking after.

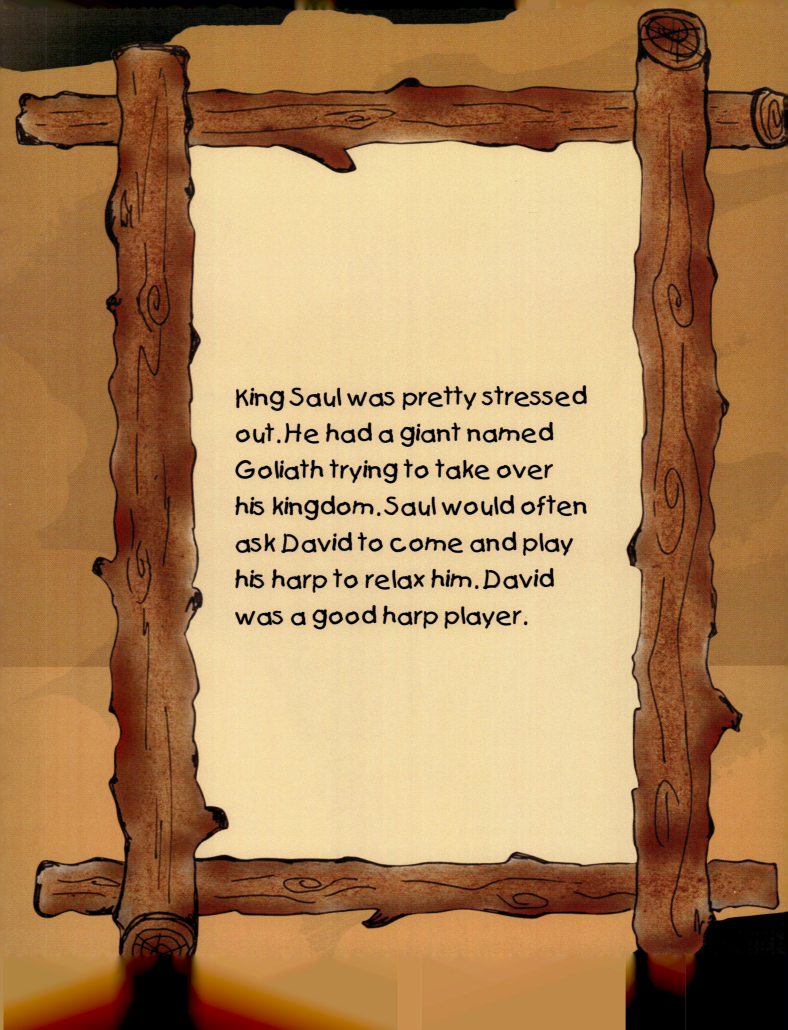

King Saul was pretty stressed
out. He had a giant named
Goliath trying to take over
his kingdom. Saul would often
ask David to come and play
his harp to relax him. David
was a good harp player.

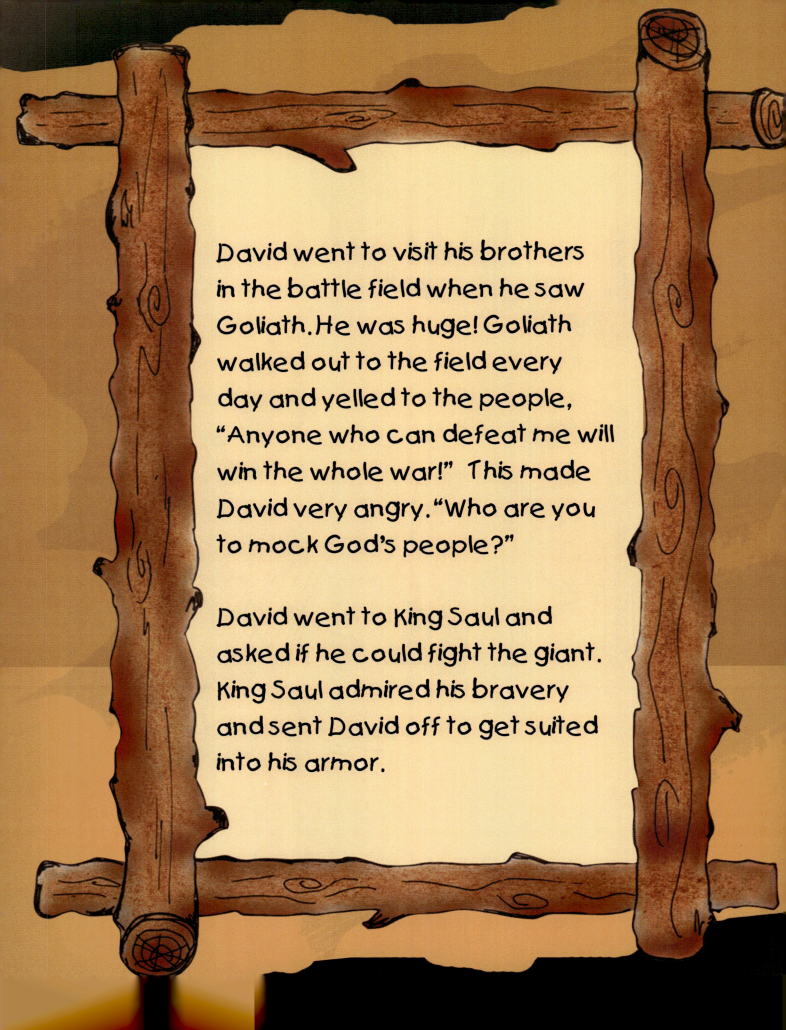

David went to visit his brothers in the battle field when he saw Goliath. He was huge! Goliath walked out to the field every day and yelled to the people, "Anyone who can defeat me will win the whole war!" This made David very angry. "Who are you to mock God's people?"

David went to King Saul and asked if he could fight the giant. King Saul admired his bravery and sent David off to get suited into his armor.

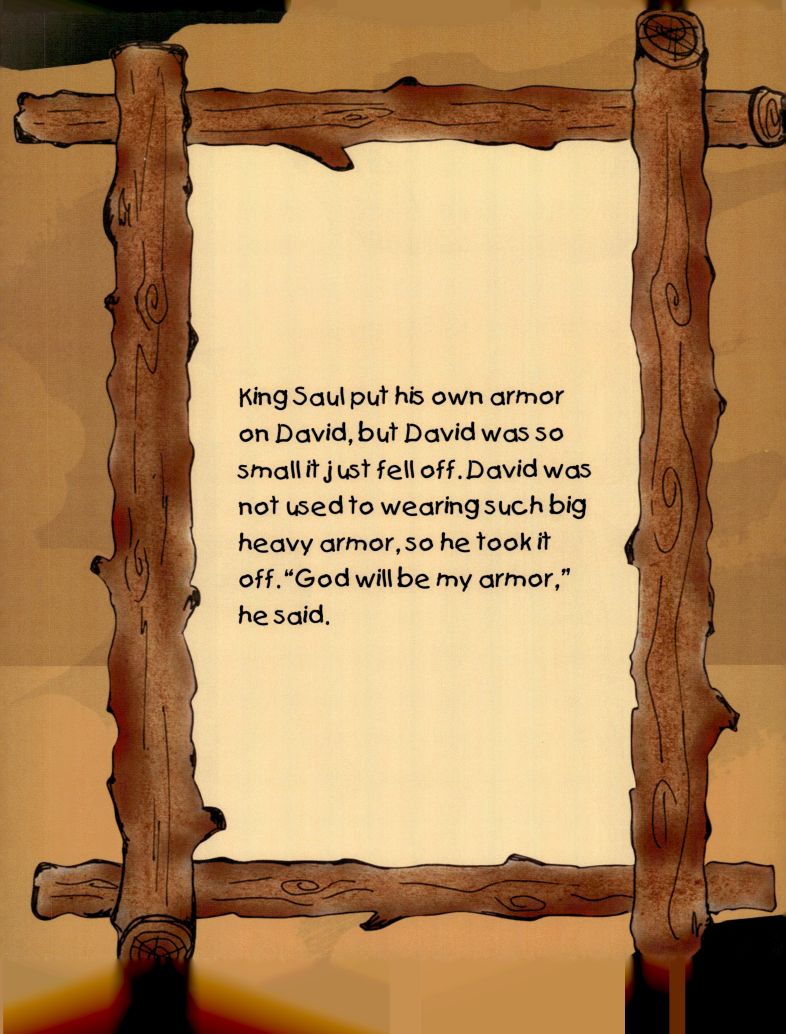

King Saul put his own armor on David, but David was so small it just fell off. David was not used to wearing such big heavy armor, so he took it off. "God will be my armor," he said.

David grabbed his slingshot, got three stones from the creek and went out to meet Goliath. Goliath almost fell over laughing when he saw how small David was. David took his sling, put a stone into it and "chucked" it at Goliath's head.

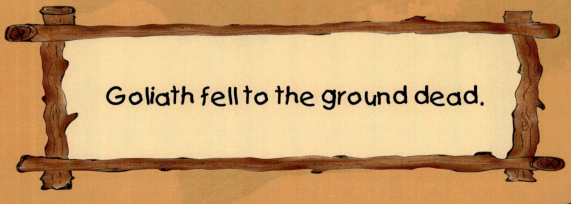

Goliath fell to the ground dead.

David's brothers and the whole army cheered God and David for defeating Goliath.

King Saul later got very jealous of David because the people liked David more than they did King Saul. Saul tried to kill David many times. King Saul chased David all over the countryside. Each time God saved David.

David would sneak up to King Saul while he was sleeping and take something of his, but he would not kill him because Saul was still God's chosen king. David would say "See, I took this while you slept instead of killing you, now please leave me alone. I do not want to hurt you."

King Saul would leave David alone for a while, but it wouldn't take long for King Saul to be running after David again.

King Saul got hung up in battle and died, God had had enough. Now David was safe from King Saul.

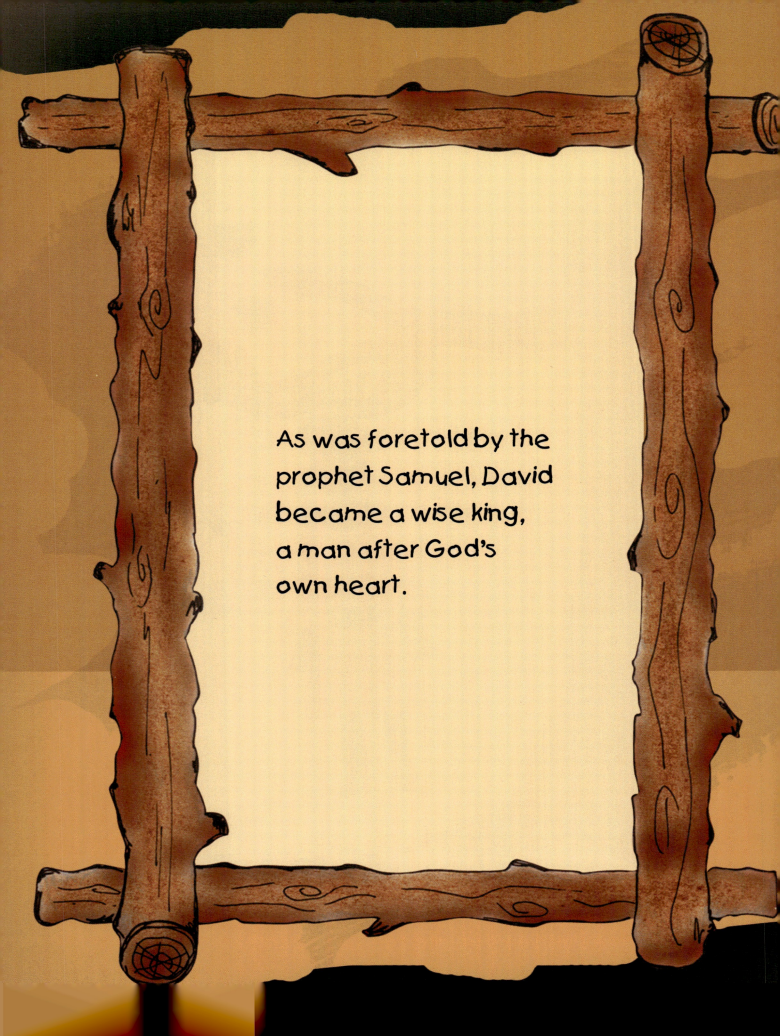

As was foretold by the prophet Samuel, David became a wise king, a man after God's own heart.

Moral of the story:

~ Watch where you are going

~ Do not be jealous of others.
  God has a different plan for
  everyone

~ Make sure you take advantage
  of all the chances God
  gives you.

The End